The

Trump-Stalin Connection

J.W. Adams

Vladimir Putin believes that the demise of the U.S.S.R. was the greatest geopolitical catastrophe of the 20th century. Veiled carefully behind that charming smile is a not-so-secret motive to bring back those "glory days." You could say his unspoken political manifesto is the Putin-equivalent to "Make America Great Again."

American President Donald Trump holds many essential traits in common with his best Russian friend, Vladimir

Putin. Leading amongst their similarities is the regular use of cartoonishly - extreme untruths as an administrative device. Putin has a genius aptitude for state-press disinformation. In 2014, after Putin's faithful officers and their state- owned machinery swarmed Ukraine, he contradicted that they were even there. His dismissal of the fact even hindered the international response and assistance extended to Ukraine. The use of intentional distortion of the truth by Putin's administration is Soviet dishonesty, once crippled for decades, now resurrected.

Stalin was also proficient at this skill, projecting an eerily Trump-esque picture of autocratic machismo, albeit with more tactful deceit. He flooded the Soviet Union with an unending supply of red herrings and many other flat-out lies that held the country hostage for many years, with a permanent creepy mustache pressed to its forehead.

Trump takes his exaggerated misrepresentations from a distinctive source, the tie-wearing, white tycoon capitalist customs of the

Western salesman. However, it merits offering a side-by-side examination of the lies in Stalin's Russia, given the unexpected invasion of Russian affairs in the Trump government.

It is a bit of an exaggeration to parallel Trump's deceptions to that of Stalin. There are many serious distinctions separating the two men. (For example, Stalin spoke deliberately, never giving the impression that he had no idea what was going on.) Trump and some of his administration seem to be impressed, even fascinated, by the

Russian approach to political gravity. For the sake of simplicity, I will focus on the fondness both of these men show for the use of deception as a rhetorical device. As we grapple through the refuse of laughable but frighteningly-real disinformation that currently plagues

Washington, D.C., we need only remember high school government to ourselves how crucial a free press is in a free society.

Political onlookers and civilians alike are disconcerted by Trump's misrepresentations and by how often he reverts to conspiracy theory whenever it suits his audience. Michael Flynn, Trump's choice for national security adviser, made his appointments quite the sideshow, backing individuals that come with bizarre backgrounds. It is unusual to see grown-ups, particularly those who are probably soon to be appointed as something important in the realm of national security, treating these odd considerations seriously.

When deceit penetrates the most important posts in the country, it pushes the people into a kind of duality. At this time in our country's history, there are literally two histories being written. In 2018, two narratives are being told in the United States, and this time it is not within the living rooms of the considerate patriot. These narratives are on television, giving every audience what they want to hear, and presenting no single American with a challenge to their ways of thinking. There are two actualities with which modern America must cope—making compromise as obsolete as the typewriter.

We are right and they are wrong. This type of thinking is not just stagnant, it is potentially lethal to freedom itself. How can our country continue to be a beacon of truth the way we were in previous generations if we lose our own grasp on the concept of truth?

Perhaps I am mistaken, but I would have to say that we lazy Americans have lost sight of the more noble goals of truth and democratic rule. The rules now include tuning into the station that agrees with you, demonizing the other side until they are practically ineffective, and breathing life into a daily political fantasy.

This is the intricate

strategy of triangulation required to wipe the slate clean on the other side of the aisle. The opposing elected leaders clearly struggle with major cognitive dissonance issues—on both sides of the aisle.

In the 1930s, Stalin was obsessed with the opposition, in particular, *a widespread network of anarchy* (as he put it) determined to remove him. Officials tortured members of the opposing party in secret and pressured them to confess to wrongdoings they did not commit. Most of them suffered official penalties that resulted in being banished to one of the labor camps across the countryside. About a million innocent people received the death penalty simply because they stood in opposition to his regime, or for much less of an offense.

The lesson is not in the horrendous number of needless deaths. In this setting, it's imperative to point out that easily-disproved inaccuracies are capable of generating devastation on a national scale. Stalin was never concerned with getting to the truth of any controversy. His main focus was always on squashing all dissent.

To its horrific end, this led to his political opponents being forced into false confessions just before being executed. The regime even started to appear lazy—showing how little they respected any drive to get to the truth—in fabricating the evidence against their political opponents. In the midst of this terror and unbelievable disregard for human life, most of the populace remained quiet and puzzled. The declaration to the people was explicit: *Update your politics. Only one political view will survive.*

Stalin often seemed like a broken record:

"Life is becoming better, my friends! Life is becoming happier!"

A talented deceiver can manipulate the masses so that they don't complain about even the most blatant and repulsive lie. There need be only a few respected voices to break through such a din, but extreme measures were taken to suppress any contrary view in the Soviet Union. The press was terrified.

While the Trumpeteers love to bash the "liberal media" even many months after the typical election-year rhetoric, not enough is said about the crucial role a free and independent media plays in a healthy democracy. Under Stalin, all news had to be authorized by party officials.

In America right now, this is far from the case. The free and independent media, a few brave Republican voices, and the majority of Americans who voted for Hillary Clinton, are watching the D.C. circus act very closely. We hope so, anyway.

Fat, lazy Americans without a healthy respect for any kind of reasonable discourse have had their day. Lovers of a free democracy will never forget that Trump regularly insults the free media. He has frequently called for the suppression of specific news organizations simply because they have opposed him. Such behavior is blatantly un-American and most obviously unpresidential.

Putin seems to maintain a respectable demeanor, even while squeezing the shit out of the free press in Russia. The American president, in his unique style, seems to do the same thing as part of a comedic gag. Is he even remotely aware that his antics never get a laugh from anyone over a certain level of political maturity? Granted, there have been many nervous laughs.

There is a very strong vein of dissatisfaction with the current president and his aloof approach to leading the world's most powerful democracy. One might say that in such uncertain times we will have a much lower tolerance if "Rocket Man" is ever actually able to deliver one of his clunky P.O.S. rockets onto an American shore. Is taunting North Korea some sort of brilliant strategy?

Please note that, no

matter how comical all of this may appear, the American public is most certainly becoming desensitized to tactics which would have been seen as major red flags in previous years. This is not the way an American president acts toward the media. It is not funny. It is quite possibly planting seeds that will haunt future elections and corrupt future presidencies.

Disinformation is rampant. In recent months, more than half of Republican voters said they believe President Trump won the 2016 popular vote in a massive landslide. He won the election, but lost the popular vote by just under 3 million votes. Political opinion is not the same thing as the truth. The line between the two has become blurrier than ever. We would be foolish to think there will be no lasting consequences.